ISBN: 9798303790186

About the Authors
In their years of working in education, the authors witnessed firsthand how technology could widen or bridge achievement gaps. Their combined experience in classroom teaching, educational technology, and equity work drives their mission to ensure AI creates positive change in education.

Introduction: The Writing of This Book

In November 2022, something extraordinary happened—a boundary dissolved between what we thought machines could do and what they could inspire in us. The release of ChatGPT marked more than just a technological leap; it offered a mirror reflecting humanity's creativity, curiosity, and occasional apprehension. These tools, far from being mere mechanical extensions of ourselves, showed their potential as collaborators—partners in rethinking the world.

This book invites you to reflect on this rethinking. It explores the historical, social, and educational dimensions of technological empowerment and exclusion, drawing striking parallels between past struggles for literacy and the pressing need for AI literacy today. It challenges us to see artificial intelligence not as a distant, abstract innovation but as a deeply human creation—shaped by our hands, powered by our imaginations, and imbued with our collective responsibility.

As you read, you'll explore perspectives on systemic inequalities and examine pathways for transformation. Each chapter invites you to critically engage with these concepts, challenge assumptions, and reflect on a pivotal question: will AI deepen existing divides, or can we leverage its potential to create a more equitable future?

This is not a step-by-step roadmap, nor is it a comprehensive guide to AI implementation in education. It does not provide technical tutorials or exhaustive policy frameworks. Instead, it seeks to inspire reflection and spark action by highlighting the urgency of AI literacy as a civil rights issue and offering broad pathways for addressing inequities in education. Readers looking for detailed curricula or technical manuals will find this book most useful as a starting point, complemented by other specialized resources.

Above all, this book aims to equip educators, administrators, and policymakers with the insights needed to think boldly, collaboratively, and inclusively in shaping a future where AI serves to uplift and empower everyone.

Enjoy the journey!

This book is not a technical manual—it is your companion in reimagining education.

AI literacy is not a luxury for the privileged

few; it is a necessity for all.

Contents

Chapter 1: Historical Parallels – Literacy and AI as Tools of Empowerment and Control

Throughout history, access to knowledge has been a contested battleground. Literacy, once withheld from marginalized communities, was a gateway to freedom, self-advocacy, and power. This chapter explores the historical denial of literacy to enslaved Black Americans as a means of oppression and control, and it draws striking parallels to today's challenges around AI access. In both cases, restricted access to crucial forms of literacy is an attempt to withhold opportunities and maintain social hierarchies.

In the 18th and 19th centuries, literacy represented a direct threat to systems of control. For enslaved Black Americans, learning to read and write was not just an educational milestone but a tool that could ignite aspirations of freedom and self-determination.

Those in power recognized this danger; as a result, laws were enacted across the Southern United States to prevent enslaved people from becoming literate. South Carolina's first anti-literacy law in 1740 imposed severe fines and imprisonment for anyone caught teaching enslaved people to read or write. The harsh penalties served as a deterrent, reinforcing a system of subjugation that kept enslaved individuals dependent, ignorant of their rights, and unable to advocate for themselves.

This control over literacy wasn't limited to enslaved people; it extended to free Black individuals as well. The South Carolina literacy law of 1834 intensified existing restrictions by including "any colored person," whether enslaved or free, under its prohibitions. This measure reflected a pervasive fear among the privileged class: if Black people could read and write, they might challenge the structures that oppressed them.

In his autobiography, Daniel Payne, an educator who became a founding member of the African Methodist Episcopal Church, described how his efforts to teach Black students in Charleston led South Carolina legislators to reinforce anti-literacy laws. To these lawmakers, Payne's work was "playing hell," a term they used to label his teaching as a radical threat to the existing order.

The stakes were high because literacy held transformative power. Frederick Douglass, a prominent abolitionist, famously asserted that literacy makes people "unfit to be a slave." Literacy was not only a skill but a pathway to understanding and resisting oppression.

Through reading and writing, individuals could communicate, organize, and build movements to challenge their condition. The laws enacted to deny literacy to Black Americans were not just about preventing education—they were about withholding power. By barring access to knowledge, those in control perpetuated a system that kept Black Americans at a social and economic disadvantage. The message was clear: literacy was dangerous because it equipped individuals with the means to challenge their oppression.

Fast forward to the 20th century, and although the explicit laws barring literacy for Black Americans were abolished, the legacy of educational inequity persisted.

Segregated schools, underfunded public education, and systemic discrimination continued to limit access to quality education for marginalized communities. The struggle for equitable access to knowledge was ongoing, with literacy remaining a symbolic and literal key to upward mobility.

By the 1970s, studies revealed that Black students were still disproportionately affected by suspensions and pushouts, perpetuating the cycle of educational deprivation. Despite the legal gains of Brown v. Board of Education in 1954, which deemed separate but equal schooling unconstitutional, the practical experiences of marginalized students showed little improvement. Schools in predominantly Black and low-income neighborhoods remained under-resourced, reinforcing the educational gaps created by centuries of exclusion.

Today, as we transition into a digital and AI-driven age, a new form of literacy is emerging: AI literacy. This form of technological proficiency is quickly becoming as essential as traditional literacy once was. AI touches every facet of modern life, from job markets to social interactions, shaping the ways we work, communicate, and even think. Proficiency in AI is now a gateway to future career opportunities and economic mobility.

However, much like literacy in the 18th and 19th centuries, access to AI literacy is unequally distributed. Schools in affluent areas are often equipped with the resources to integrate AI education, while underfunded schools—disproportionately located in Black, Brown, and low-income communities—are left without the means to provide this critical knowledge.

This exclusion from AI literacy mirrors the historical denial of traditional literacy. By limiting AI education, schools deprive marginalized students of the skills necessary to participate fully in an AI-driven society.

Without access to AI, students in these communities are at risk of being relegated to the margins, much as their ancestors were when they were denied access to literacy. They may find themselves controlled by AI systems rather than being able to understand, use, and shape these technologies.

The impact of this exclusion is profound: just as literacy bans kept Black Americans from the social and economic benefits of education, AI exclusion today threatens to keep students who are marginalized out of future high-paying, innovative industries.

AI literacy is a new civil rights issue. Denying marginalized communities access to AI education replicates the exclusionary practices of the past, where literacy was withheld to keep people powerless. The societal implications of this exclusion are profound. AI is not just a technological tool; it represents an entry point to the modern world. AI literacy, defined as the comprehensive ability to understand, critically evaluate, and ethically engage with artificial intelligence technologies, has become as crucial as traditional literacy. This multifaceted skill encompasses technical comprehension, critical thinking, and ethical awareness, enabling individuals to not just consume AI technologies but to understand, shape, and potentially transform them

In an AI-driven economy, those without AI literacy risk being confined to low-skill, low-wage jobs, unable to access the social mobility that AI offers. The divide between those who can understand and control AI and those who cannot is widening, and it threatens to create a new form of economic and social stratification.

Understanding this historical context of literacy exclusion allows us to recognize the urgency of ensuring equitable access to AI education today. AI literacy is not a luxury for the privileged few; it is a necessity for all, especially those who have historically been denied access to empowering tools and knowledge.

By framing AI literacy as a civil rights issue, we set the stage for a broader conversation on how to prevent repeating the mistakes of the past. Instead of allowing AI to reinforce inequalities, we have an opportunity to harness its power as a tool for equity and empowerment, ensuring that marginalized communities have the chance to learn, use, and shape AI in ways that serve their interests and uplift their voices.

AI Literacy as a Path to Equity

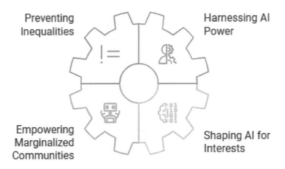

Preventing Inequalities

Harnessing AI Power

Empowering Marginalized Communities

Shaping AI for Interests

While literacy laws once restricted access to knowledge, today's barriers to AI literacy create similar divisions. These modern restrictions manifest in various ways, shaping how different communities engage with AI technology.

The next chapters will delve into the specifics of this challenge—how marginalized communities are being excluded from AI literacy, the impacts of this exclusion, and the potential of AI to act as a tool for empowerment if integrated equitably into education.

Chapter 2: AI as the New Literacy – The Impact of Exclusion on Marginalized Communities

The parallel between historical literacy barriers and modern AI access isn't just symbolic—it's systemic. As crucial as reading and writing in today's digital world, AI literacy encompasses the ability to understand, critically evaluate, interact with, and ethically engage with artificial intelligence technologies. As AI shapes every facet of society, understanding and navigating this technology is vital for economic opportunity and social mobility. Yet, just as literacy was historically denied to marginalized communities, access to AI education is now uneven, with underfunded schools often lacking the resources to teach AI.

This chapter delves into the impact of AI exclusion on marginalized communities, drawing on historical parallels with literacy, examining the concept of "reasonable reluctance" toward AI, and proposing solutions to ensure that all students can build AI literacy.

Historically, literacy has been equated with power. Access to reading and writing enabled individuals to pursue knowledge, economic advancement, and self-advocacy. Figures like Frederick Douglass understood that literacy was a gateway to freedom, as Douglass pursued reading and writing despite legal and social barriers. Today, AI literacy holds similar significance. The ability to understand and use AI is becoming indispensable, with parallels to traditional literacy as a means to social mobility and empowerment.

Yet disadvantaged communities, who have long faced educational barriers, are again at risk of being excluded from this critical skill. Denying access to AI is akin to past literacy restrictions, perpetuating a cycle of educational inequity that keeps marginalized students from fully participating in the modern economy.

AI exclusion today can be seen in the restrictions some schools place on AI use, often viewing it as a "cheating" tool rather than an educational resource. In many underfunded schools, AI tools are either banned or heavily regulated, reinforcing a divide between schools with access to advanced technology and those without. While wealthier districts integrate AI tools into the curriculum, preparing students for AI-driven careers, underfunded schools often lack the necessary infrastructure, devices, and high-speed internet access to support AI education.

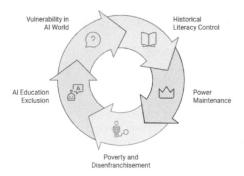

The Cycle of Exclusion and Oppression

Vulnerability in AI World · Historical Literacy Control · AI Education Exclusion · Power Maintenance · Poverty and Disenfranchisement

The disparity between AI-rich and AI-poor educational settings creates an alarming new digital divide, leaving oppressed students at a disadvantage in an economy that increasingly values technological fluency.

Another layer to this exclusion is the concept of "reasonable reluctance" within marginalized communities. Due to historical and systemic inequities, Black and Brown students often face more scrutiny when using generative technologies like AI, with their work subjected to accusations of dishonesty or "cheating" more frequently than their white peers. This suspicion leads to a negative perception of AI in these communities, reinforcing a fear of engaging with technology.

This reluctance stems from a long history of educational barriers, punitive measures, and a lack of trust in systems that have historically alienated these communities. Terms associated with AI detection, such as "tracking" and "detecting," carry a punitive connotation that can discourage students from exploring AI tools. Without targeted support to overcome this hesitation, students may exclude themselves from using AI, missing out on a crucial literacy that is increasingly required for future success.

One approach to countering this reluctance is implementing a Significant Human Authorship (SHA) policy within educational institutions. A

SHA policy formalizes AI use within academic work, providing clear guidelines on how students can ethically incorporate AI tools into their learning. The SHA policy supports "assumption of use," where AI's presence in student work is accepted as a learning tool rather than treated with suspicion.

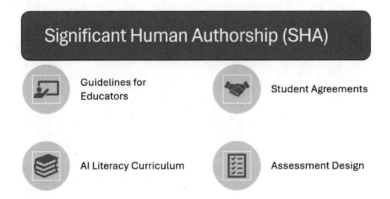

Significant Human Authorship (SHA)

Guidelines for Educators

Student Agreements

AI Literacy Curriculum

Assessment Design

This approach aligns with the U.S. Copyright Office's March 2023 decision to permit works with minimal AI input to be copyright-protected if human authorship is significant. By establishing this policy, schools can protect students from accusations of dishonesty and create an environment where AI is an accessible, trusted tool for all students.

Importantly, an SHA policy also empowers marginalized students to engage with AI confidently, knowing that their use of the technology is recognized as legitimate and valuable.

The absence of a formal policy on AI use can lead to what's called a "ghost policy" that affects students differently based on their school's resources or attitudes toward AI. Schools that lack an official stance on AI use risk creating inconsistent and discriminatory practices, where students in "good" schools or districts with forward-thinking superintendents have access to AI, while those in under-resourced schools do not. This creates an equity issue, where students' access to AI depends more on their school's policies than on their educational needs.

Implementing a SHA policy and shifting to an "assumption of use" can eliminate these discrepancies, ensuring that all students can use AI tools without fear of unfair consequences.

Beyond formal policies, viewing AI literacy as a fundamental right for all students is essential, akin to reading and writing. Denying minority students access to AI keeps them passive consumers of technology, rather than active participants and innovators.

Research shows that AI proficiency will be critical for future careers in nearly every sector, from healthcare to finance. Without access to AI, vulnerable students will struggle to compete in the job market and may find themselves relegated to low-skill, low-wage jobs while their more privileged counterparts secure leadership roles in an AI-driven economy.

This exclusion is not just an educational gap; it is a systemic barrier to social and economic mobility.

An empowering shift in AI literacy requires schools to foster a supportive environment where students from all backgrounds can explore AI without fear of punishment or suspicion. Schools can achieve this by promoting AI as a skill that enhances critical thinking, creativity, and ethical understanding.

By normalizing AI use, particularly within communities with historical hesitations around new technologies, educational institutions can help students develop confidence in using AI as a tool for growth. Engaging with AI literacy gives students the power to question, challenge, and even shape the technology that impacts their lives.

This level of engagement is essential for fostering a future workforce that reflects diverse experiences and perspectives, creating AI tools that are inclusive, fair, and representative.

For marginalized students, AI literacy can also serve as a tool of empowerment and self-advocacy. As students from underrepresented backgrounds learn to understand and work with AI, they gain a sense of agency over the technology shaping the world around them.

This empowerment allows them not only to compete for high-paying jobs but also to contribute their unique perspectives to the development of AI. With greater representation in AI-related fields, these students can help address biases that exist within AI systems, ensuring that future technologies are developed with a broader range of human experiences in mind. This inclusive approach to AI has the potential to make technology fairer and more attuned to the needs of diverse communities.

AI literacy is more than just a technological skill; it is a pathway to economic inclusion, social mobility, and empowerment. By addressing the barriers to AI access, implementing formal policies like Significant Human Authorship, and fostering a supportive culture around AI use, schools can ensure that AI literacy is accessible to all students.

Policymakers, educators, and community leaders must work together to close the digital divide, transforming AI from a source of inequality into a tool for equity. This commitment to AI literacy for all will allow neglected students to not only navigate but also shape the AI-driven world, making it more just, inclusive, and representative. As we prioritize AI literacy, we must remember that access to technology isn't a privilege—it's a fundamental right for participation in tomorrow's economy and society.

Chapter 3: Adapting to Change – AI's Role in Evolving Career Paths

Artificial intelligence is fundamentally altering the global job market. A 2024 Microsoft study revealed that 75% of international knowledge workers are already using AI in their daily tasks, with usage doubling in just six months. This rapid adoption signifies more than a fad— it reshapes how we work, who thrives, and what skills are deemed essential.

Alarmingly, 66% of leaders now state they would not hire someone without AI skills, highlighting that AI literacy has transitioned from being a competitive advantage to a fundamental requirement for accessing high-paying jobs and achieving economic mobility. Over the past four decades, the wealth gap has widened, as slower wage growth for Black Americans and higher rates of asset appreciation for White Americans have compounded inequality, according to the National Bureau of Economic Research.

This growing disparity raises profound questions about equity. Throughout history, access to transformative skills—whether literacy in the 19th century or coding in the 21st—has determined who wields power and who is left behind. AI has now joined this lineage, shattering traditional career ceilings for those who can access its opportunities while erecting new barriers for those who cannot. In this shifting landscape, adaptability and AI literacy are no longer optional; they are essential for ensuring broad and inclusive participation in the future economy.

The stakes are high. If equitable access to AI education and tools isn't prioritized, we risk perpetuating cycles of exclusion that parallel historical denials of literacy. By recognizing AI literacy as a critical civil right, we can ensure that this technological transformation uplifts rather than excludes, creating a future of work that is inclusive, just, and reflective of our collective potential.

Artificial intelligence (AI) is reshaping the global job market, transforming traditional career paths, and creating new demands for adaptability. As AI continues to impact nearly every industry, individuals from marginalized communities face unique challenges in navigating this rapidly changing landscape. Historically, technological advancements have reshaped work and often left the most vulnerable workers at a disadvantage, and the shift to an AI-driven economy threatens to do the same if not addressed equitably. This chapter examines how AI is changing career paths, the need for adaptability, and the implications for disadvantaged communities striving to remain competitive in this new landscape.

Throughout history, major technological shifts have created both opportunities and disruptions. The Industrial Revolution, for example, transformed the economy from one based on handicrafts and agriculture to one centered on machines and manufacturing. This change was devastating for many skilled tradespeople whose work was replaced by machines, while creating a demand for workers who could operate and manage these machines. Knowledge and education became more valuable than physical skill in many industries, marking a major turning point in the nature of work. As the industrial economy evolved, those who adapted to new demands thrived, while others were left behind.

Today, we are witnessing a similar shift. AI and automation are revolutionizing workplaces, creating a need for new skills while rendering certain roles obsolete. LinkedIn has speculated that more than half of its members may see their jobs altered or eliminated due to AI advancements.

Studies suggest that white-collar jobs—once considered stable and prestigious—are among the most vulnerable to AI's impact. From customer service to legal research, tasks that were once handled by humans are now increasingly managed by AI systems. As a result, those in traditional corporate or administrative roles must adapt quickly, developing new skills to remain relevant in a workforce that prioritizes technological fluency.

For marginalized communities, this shift presents significant challenges. Many individuals from these communities have followed conventional career pathways, often investing time, money, and effort to build expertise in fields now being reshaped by AI.

Imagine a worker who has spent decades in a white-collar role, only to find that their position is now redundant due to AI advancements. Adapting to these changes can be particularly daunting for those with limited financial resources or educational opportunities. They may lack access to the training programs, mentorship, or technology needed to learn new skills and transition into AI-relevant fields. As such, AI's impact on traditional career paths risks exacerbating existing inequalities, with marginalized workers facing greater difficulty in adapting to new demands.

One of the biggest challenges in this transformation is the pace of change. The speed at which AI is advancing has made it difficult for both workers and institutions to keep up. The idea of "job security" is increasingly uncertain, with reports showing that roles in fields like social media management, data entry, and customer support are already being automated.

While some blue-collar jobs are less immediately affected, AI-driven automation is also starting to enter sectors like retail and fast food, with AI-enabled systems handling tasks traditionally done by humans. In fast food restaurants, for example, AI "bots" can take orders, interpret non-verbal cues, and provide a seamless customer experience. As these technologies become more sophisticated and affordable, employers are likely to adopt them in favor of human workers, reducing labor costs and improving efficiency.

This rapid technological evolution means that adaptability is no longer optional; it is essential. Workers who wish to thrive in an AI-driven economy must develop skills that complement AI, rather than compete with it. This includes critical thinking, creativity, emotional intelligence, and complex problem-solving—skills that are uniquely human and difficult to replicate with AI.

Disadvantaged communities often face barriers to developing these skills. For many students in underfunded schools, access to resources that would enable them to explore AI and build these competencies is limited. As a result, they are at risk of being left behind in a job market that increasingly values technological proficiency.

AI's impact on career paths also raises questions about the value of traditional education. For decades, obtaining a college degree has been considered the best route to financial stability and career advancement.

However, with AI transforming the job landscape, a college degree alone may no longer guarantee economic security. In fact, some studies suggest that AI is impacting white-collar and professional roles at a faster rate than trade or technical jobs.

As AI technology advances, individuals who are skilled in operating AI systems or who possess hands-on skills that are less easily automated may find themselves in greater demand than those with conventional degrees. For oppressed communities, this shift may provide both challenges and opportunities: while it could open pathways into high-demand technical fields, it also requires a reevaluation of educational priorities to focus on skills that are compatible with an AI-driven economy.

Adapting to an AI-driven job market requires a mindset shift as well as skill development. The transition from manual labor to industrial labor during the Industrial Revolution created what we now recognize as a modern work culture, with expectations around wages, working hours, and benefits. Similarly, the AI revolution is challenging existing notions of career progression, with AI-enabled roles often emphasizing flexibility, project-based work, and continuous learning. Workers in marginalized communities may need to adapt to this evolving model of employment, which prioritizes ongoing skill development over long-term job security.

This requires access to lifelong learning opportunities, including training programs, apprenticeships, and online courses, yet access to these resources remains limited in many underserved areas.

Moreover, disadvantaged communities may experience unique forms of vulnerability in adapting to AI-driven changes. Some workers in traditionally human-centered roles may find that their roles are devalued as AI systems take on tasks that were once thought to require human empathy, intuition, or complex decision-making. The integration of AI into workplaces has introduced profound changes, with layoffs becoming a stark indicator of these shifts. For instance, Boeing, KPMG, and General Motors announced significant layoffs in Q4 2024, impacting thousands of lives and reshaping job landscapes. Marginalized communities, in particular, may face unique vulnerabilities as they navigate these AI-driven disruptions. Roles traditionally centered on human skills—empathy, intuition, and complex decision-making—are increasingly devalued as AI systems take on tasks once believed to require these qualities.

For example, customer service positions, which have historically relied on interpersonal communication, are rapidly being replaced by AI chatbots designed to understand and respond to customer needs. This transition not only displaces workers but can also have deep emotional and psychological consequences. Workers may feel a loss of identity and value, as skills they once considered uniquely human are now rendered redundant by machines. This sense of displacement is particularly acute in communities where access to alternative opportunities and resources is already limited, compounding existing inequities.

Customer service roles, which often rely on interpersonal communication skills, are increasingly being replaced by AI chatbots capable of understanding and responding to customer needs. This not only displaces workers but can also create emotional and psychological impacts, as individuals may feel that their unique human skills are no longer valued.

Without access to training and resources to adapt, these workers face the risk of becoming marginalized in a job market that prioritizes technological proficiency over personal experience and interpersonal skills.

The Impact of AI on Customer Service

Psychological Impact — Mental effects of AI integration

Emotional Impact — Feelings of devaluation and loss

Job Displacement — The replacement of human roles with AI

Adapting to an AI-driven economy also demands financial resilience, which can be difficult for individuals in neglected communities. AI technology often requires expensive infrastructure, access to digital tools, and high-speed internet—resources that are not always available to low-income individuals or underfunded schools.

Marginalized individuals, who may already struggle with financial insecurity, could find it challenging to invest in the training and technology needed to stay competitive. This disparity reinforces the economic divide, leaving those without resources at a disadvantage.

For these communities, AI literacy is not just a skill but a means of economic survival, a way to remain relevant in a world that is moving towards automation and digital innovation at a rapid pace.

AI is reshaping career paths in ways that both challenge and empower individuals. For oppressed communities, however, the path forward is filled with obstacles. The rapid pace of technological change, coupled with limited access to AI education and resources, threatens to leave these communities behind.

As AI becomes a defining force in the global economy, it is essential to ensure that all individuals have the tools to adapt and thrive. Policymakers, educators, and community leaders must recognize the unique challenges facing marginalized communities and work to provide equitable access to AI training, resources, and support.

Without these interventions, AI's impact on career paths will continue to deepen existing inequalities, restricting economic mobility for those who are already disadvantaged.

The journey of adapting to AI is not just about preparing for new types of jobs; it is about redefining the future of work and ensuring that it is inclusive for everyone.

By investing in AI literacy, particularly for those who have historically been marginalized, we can create a workforce that is not only capable of thriving in an AI-driven world but is also empowered to shape it. This transformation begins in our classrooms.

Chapter 4: AI as a Tool for Equity – Harnessing Its Potential for Inclusive Education

Artificial intelligence is emerging as a powerful equalizer in education, enabling personalized learning and helping to close achievement gaps for marginalized communities. With thoughtful integration, AI can support underfunded schools by providing tailored assistance that empowers all students to succeed.

A recent Harvard study (under peer review) found that students using an AI tutor based on sound pedagogical principles doubled their learning gains in less time compared to traditional methods. This highlights the transformative potential of AI to reshape how education is designed, delivered, and experienced when implemented thoughtfully.

Realizing this potential requires an intentional shift in how we approach AI in education. Rather than seeing AI as a threat, we must view it as a tool that, when used responsibly, can create more equitable and inclusive learning environments. This chapter examines the opportunities AI presents for education equity, the specific benefits it can bring to vulnerable students, and the responsibility of educators and policymakers to ensure equitable access to AI-powered resources.

One of the most transformative aspects of AI in education is its ability to personalize learning experiences. Traditional teaching methods are often one-size-fits-all, which can leave students with diverse needs struggling to keep up or feeling unchallenged. AI-powered educational tools, however, can adapt to each student's unique learning style, pace, and strengths.

For example, AI-driven programs can analyze students' performance in real-time, identifying areas where they need additional support or practice. This approach allows teachers to provide differentiated instruction, ensuring that each student receives the guidance they need to succeed.

In underfunded schools, where teachers often manage large class sizes and limited resources, AI can act as a support system, helping teachers deliver more personalized education even when resources are stretched thin.

For marginalized students, AI's capacity for personalized learning offers a lifeline to academic success. Many students in low-income or under-resourced schools face barriers that go beyond the classroom, including limited access to learning materials, support systems, and extracurricular opportunities.

AI can help bridge these gaps by providing individualized educational experiences that cater to each student's needs. For instance, an AI tutoring program could assist a student struggling with math, offering practice problems, explanations, and feedback tailored to their level of understanding.

This individualized attention is particularly valuable in schools where teachers may not have the capacity to provide one-on-one support for every student. By giving marginalized students the tools to learn at their own pace and gain mastery in critical areas, AI can empower them to compete academically with peers from more advantaged backgrounds.

AI also has the potential to support educators in addressing diverse learning needs. In many under-resourced schools, teachers are tasked with meeting the needs of students with widely varying abilities, language backgrounds, and learning challenges. AI can assist by offering tools for language translation, assisting with special education needs, and adapting content to make it accessible for all students.

For example, AI-powered language translation tools can help English language learners (ELL) by translating instructions or reading materials, allowing them to engage fully in the classroom while improving their English skills. Similarly, AI tools designed to assist students with disabilities can enable these learners to access content in ways that work best for them, whether through text-to-speech software, visual aids, or interactive simulations. In this way, AI can help level the playing field, ensuring that students from marginalized backgrounds or those with specific learning needs have the support necessary to succeed.

Teaching AI literacy can have far-reaching effects beyond immediate academic performance. When students learn to use and understand AI, they gain skills that are increasingly valuable in the workforce and society at large. For marginalized communities, this access to AI literacy is particularly transformative. Learning AI provides students with the opportunity to become not just consumers of technology but creators and innovators. When students from diverse backgrounds understand AI, they can bring their unique perspectives to its development and application, helping to create technology that better serves all communities.

Path to AI Empowerment

Transform Communities

The impact of AI literacy leads to positive changes in communities.

Innovate with Perspectives

Diverse students contribute unique ideas to AI development.

Create Technology

Students apply their skills to develop new AI applications.

Develop Skills

Students enhance their technical skills through practice and projects.

Learn AI Basics

Students begin by understanding fundamental AI concepts.

This inclusion is especially important given the biases that can exist in AI systems, which often reflect the perspectives of those who create them. By equipping marginalized students with AI skills, we enable them to participate in shaping the future of technology, fostering a tech industry that is more representative, equitable, and mindful of diverse experiences and needs.

Despite AI's potential to promote equity, many marginalized communities lack access to these tools and resources. Underfunded schools often face significant barriers in adopting new technologies, from financial limitations to lack of infrastructure and training.

For instance, implementing AI-powered learning tools requires high-speed internet, up-to-date devices, and teachers who are trained to use these tools effectively. Schools in affluent districts may have these resources, while those in low-income areas are frequently left without, perpetuating the cycle of educational inequality.

To bridge this gap, policymakers and educational institutions must prioritize equitable access to AI, allocating funds and resources to schools that need it most. Without these interventions, AI will only reinforce existing divides, leaving marginalized students without the tools they need to succeed in an AI-driven world.

Beyond access to technology, teacher training is critical to maximizing AI's potential in education. Even when AI tools are available, teachers must know how to use them effectively to support student learning. In underfunded schools, teachers often lack access to professional development opportunities, meaning they may not have the skills to incorporate AI into their classrooms.

Investing in teacher training is essential to ensure that AI is used as a tool for inclusion rather than exclusion. Educators need training not only in the technical aspects of AI but also in ethical considerations, such as data privacy and bias, to ensure that AI is used responsibly. By equipping teachers with the knowledge to integrate AI thoughtfully and effectively, we can ensure that all students benefit from this technology.

The potential of AI in education extends beyond supporting individual student achievement—it can also foster a sense of agency and innovation among marginalized students. When students understand AI and its applications, they gain the power to question, influence, and shape the technology that impacts their lives.

For marginalized communities, this empowerment is vital. Too often, technology is created without consideration for diverse perspectives, leading to AI systems that can perpetuate biases or exclude certain groups.

By teaching AI literacy to all students, we can encourage a generation of learners who not only use AI but contribute to its development in ways that reflect and respect diverse experiences. This shift in perspective transforms AI from a passive tool into an active platform for advocacy, innovation, and representation.

AI has the potential to be a powerful tool for equity in education, helping to bridge long-standing gaps and empower marginalized students with the skills they need to succeed in a digital world.

This requires investments in technology, teacher training, and supportive infrastructure, particularly for under-resourced schools.

Policymakers and educational leaders must recognize that AI literacy is a fundamental right, essential for participating in an increasingly AI-driven society.

By bridging the AI divide, we can create an educational system that truly serves every student and prepares them for a future where technology is an integral part of everyday life. This transformation requires clear strategies and systemic support.

The next chapter will explore the actions necessary to achieve this vision, calling upon educators, policymakers, and communities to commit to AI literacy as an essential component of equity and inclusion in the modern world. Only by bridging the AI divide can we create an educational system that truly serves every student and prepares them for a future where technology is an integral part of everyday life.

Chapter 5: Components for Success: Equity first

Artificial intelligence will become ubiquitous, and ensuring accessibility demands concrete action and infrastructure.   It is critical that educators, policymakers, and communities prioritize AI literacy for all students, emphasizing the urgency of providing marginalized communities with the tools to thrive in an AI-driven world.

Equitable access to AI literacy is vital because it empowers students from all backgrounds to participate fully in the future workforce and society. Schools that fail to provide AI education are effectively depriving their students of the skills necessary to succeed in an AI-driven economy. This exclusion not only limits individual potential but also perpetuates systemic inequalities that keep marginalized communities from advancing economically and socially. Access to AI education must therefore be recognized as a fundamental right, not a privilege reserved for well-funded schools.

One of the first steps in achieving equitable AI literacy is removing bans and restrictions on AI in educational settings. Many schools today view AI with suspicion, seeing it as a potential distraction or as a shortcut that undermines traditional learning. However, by banning AI or limiting its use, schools are denying students access to a tool that is crucial for their future.

Rather than treating AI as a threat, educators should view it as an opportunity to teach students about ethical, responsible, and creative AI use. By integrating AI thoughtfully into the curriculum, schools can prepare students to engage with this technology in a way that is both productive and ethical. Educators must shift the narrative around AI from one of fear and restriction to one of empowerment and possibility.

To implement AI education effectively, policymakers and school districts must invest in the necessary infrastructure and resources, particularly for underfunded schools. AI tools require up-to-date technology, high-speed internet, and ongoing maintenance, resources that are often lacking in low-income school districts. Without these investments, AI literacy will remain out of reach for many students.

Allocating funds specifically for AI resources in under-resourced schools is essential to close the digital divide. This could include providing computers and tablets equipped with AI tools, upgrading internet capabilities, and ensuring that every student has access to digital learning environments that support AI education.

Teacher training is another critical component in achieving equitable AI literacy. Even in schools where AI tools are available, teachers must be equipped with the knowledge and confidence to use them effectively.

Professional development programs focused on AI should be accessible to all educators, regardless of the resources of their school district. Training should cover both the technical aspects of AI tools and ethical considerations, such as data privacy, bias, and responsible AI use.

By empowering teachers with the skills they need to integrate AI in the classroom, schools can create a learning environment that fosters curiosity, creativity, and critical thinking around technology. Educators who understand AI's potential can become advocates for its responsible use, helping students see AI not as a threat but as a powerful tool they can control and shape.

Developing a curriculum that includes AI literacy is essential for preparing students for the future. AI literacy should not be limited to technical skills but should include an understanding of the ethical, social, and economic implications of AI. Schools can create interdisciplinary AI curricula that cover topics such as the history of AI, how AI impacts different sectors, and the societal challenges posed by automation and AI bias.

This approach allows students to see AI in a broader context, understanding not only how it works but also how it affects society. Lessons on ethical AI use, for example, can encourage students to think critically about issues like surveillance, data privacy, and algorithmic bias, fostering a generation of informed citizens who can engage thoughtfully with technology.

Engaging with AI also provides marginalized students with a unique opportunity to shape the future of technology. By equipping students from diverse backgrounds with AI literacy, we are helping to diversify the voices and perspectives involved in AI development.

Representation in technology is essential to address the biases that can be embedded in AI systems, as AI often reflects the viewpoints of those who create it. When marginalized students learn to understand and develop AI, they bring their own experiences and insights, challenging and expanding the ways AI is applied. This inclusivity in AI development has the potential to lead to fairer, more representative, and more effective AI systems that serve a broader range of communities.

In addition to these educational efforts, a broader commitment to community engagement is needed to support AI literacy. Schools can partner with local organizations, businesses, and tech companies to provide resources, mentorship, and real-world learning opportunities for students.

Community workshops and AI literacy programs aimed at parents and families can help demystify AI, addressing fears and misconceptions about the technology. Involving families in AI literacy initiatives not only broadens the reach of these efforts but also fosters a community-wide understanding of the importance of AI. By creating a culture that values AI literacy, communities can support their schools in building an inclusive foundation for future generations.

Finally, policymakers play a crucial role in ensuring that AI literacy is prioritized at all levels of government. State and federal education departments must recognize AI as an essential component of modern education and provide guidance and funding to support its integration.

Policymakers can enact legislation that mandates AI literacy in school curricula, ensuring that all students, regardless of their background, have the opportunity to learn about this critical technology. Funding initiatives, grants, and policy changes can make AI literacy programs sustainable, providing long-term support for schools as they work to close the digital divide.

By championing AI literacy as a civil rights issue, policymakers can drive systemic change that empowers marginalized communities with the tools to succeed in an AI-driven world.

Equitable access to AI literacy is a pressing need in today's world. By removing bans, investing in resources and infrastructure, training educators, developing inclusive curricula, and engaging communities, we can create an educational system that serves all students and prepares them for the opportunities and challenges of an AI-driven society.

It is not enough to simply introduce AI tools in classrooms; we must ensure that these tools are accessible, understood, and used in ways that empower all students. While policy frameworks are essential, their success depends on effective classroom implementation. Teachers stand at the forefront of this transformation.

Chapter 6: Practical Steps: Building AI Literacy in the Classroom

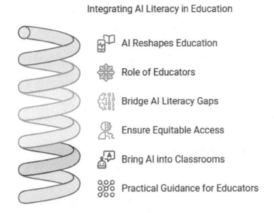

Integrating AI Literacy in Education

- AI Reshapes Education
- Role of Educators
- Bridge AI Literacy Gaps
- Ensure Equitable Access
- Bring AI into Classrooms
- Practical Guidance for Educators

As AI reshapes the landscape of education, the role of educators becomes pivotal. Teachers are not merely facilitators of knowledge; they are architects of opportunity. To bridge the gaps in AI literacy and ensure equitable access, educators must take actionable steps to bring AI into classrooms, not as a distant or intimidating technology but as a tool for empowerment and inclusion. Building on the systemic strategies outlined in **Chapter 5,** this chapter provides practical guidance for educators and leaders ready to embrace this challenge.

Integrating AI into the classroom does not require a complete overhaul of teaching practices. Start small. Identify a specific lesson or topic where AI can enhance learning outcomes. For example, you could use AI-powered writing tools like Grammarly to provide real-time feedback on grammar and style, or Quizlet to generate personalized quizzes that adapt to students' needs. These tools not only support learning but also introduce students to AI in a way that feels natural and relevant.

Encourage students to engage with AI hands-on. For instance, in a writing assignment, students might use ChatGPT to brainstorm essay ideas. Then, guide them in critically analyzing the AI's suggestions: What did the AI do well? What did it miss? How could they refine the AI's output to make it more useful? Exercises like these teach students not only how to use AI but also how to think critically about its capabilities and limitations—a skill that will be essential in an AI-driven world.

Actionable Steps:

- Introduce one AI tool that aligns with your curriculum.
- Create an activity that encourages students to evaluate AI outputs critically.
- Provide clear instructions and examples to build confidence in using AI tools.

Addressing Equity Challenges
Systemic inequities often limit access to AI tools and technologies. As an educator, you can play a vital role in addressing these disparities. Start by assessing the resources your students have at home and in the classroom. For those who lack devices or internet access, advocate for solutions like loaner laptops, mobile hotspots, or additional school lab time.

Partner with local businesses, nonprofits, or community organizations to secure funding for AI tools and infrastructure. Many companies offer grants for educational technology—seek them out. Additionally, normalize AI use in your classroom through inclusive policies that emphasize its role as a learning aid, not a shortcut. For example, establish guidelines for when and how students can use AI in assignments, ensuring that it is seen as a complement to their skills, not a replacement.

Actionable Steps:

- Audit your classroom resources to identify gaps in technology access.
- Research and apply for grants to bring AI tools to your school.
- Develop classroom policies that promote equitable access and ethical AI use.

Investing in Professional Development
Teachers need the skills and confidence to integrate AI effectively. Begin by exploring free or low-cost resources tailored for educators. Platforms like the Microsoft Educator Center or LinkedIn Learning offer beginner-friendly courses on topics like AI basics, ethical use, and classroom integration.

Collaboration is another powerful tool. Form local teacher groups or join online communities focused on AI literacy. These networks allow you to share best practices, discuss challenges, and learn from others' experiences. Professional development isn't just about gaining new skills—it's about building a support system that helps you navigate the evolving demands of AI in education.

Actionable Steps:

- Dedicate a few hours per month to exploring professional development resources.
- Partner with other educators to share strategies for integrating AI.
- Advocate for district-wide AI training initiatives.

Promoting Ethical AI Use

As AI becomes more embedded in education, its ethical implications must be openly discussed. Use your classroom as a space to explore these questions. For example, present real-world scenarios like biased hiring algorithms or the use of AI in surveillance. Ask students to consider: What are the potential benefits of these applications? What are the risks? How can we ensure AI is used responsibly?

Model ethical AI use in your own practices. When you use AI to prepare lesson plans or generate student feedback, be transparent about it. Explain how the AI contributed to your work and why you chose to use it. This not only sets an example for students but also builds trust in AI as a tool that enhances, rather than replaces, human effort.

Actionable Steps:

- Facilitate classroom discussions on AI ethics using real-world examples.
- Introduce students to key concepts like bias, transparency, and accountability in AI.
- Demonstrate responsible AI use in your teaching practices.

Inspiring Students to Shape AI

Beyond teaching students to use AI, inspire them to shape its future. Encourage creative projects where students can build or customize AI tools. For example, they could design a chatbot to answer FAQs about your school, create AI-generated art, or analyze data from a class survey using simple coding platforms.

Connect these activities to real-world opportunities. Bring in guest speakers from AI-driven industries, organize virtual career panels, or assign research projects on how AI is transforming various fields. By linking AI to students' career aspirations, you help them see themselves as active participants in the AI revolution.

Actionable Steps:

- Create projects where students use AI tools creatively.
- Highlight AI's role in real-world industries through guest speakers or career research.

- Encourage students to explore AI's potential to solve local or global challenges.

The Educator's Role in Shaping the Future
Teachers hold a unique power to transform AI literacy from an abstract idea into a tangible, lived experience for their students. By taking even small steps, educators can create ripple effects that expand opportunities, particularly for those in marginalized communities. The path forward demands creativity, persistence, and collaboration. It is not about mastering every aspect of AI overnight but about starting the journey—together. As an educator, you are not just preparing students to adapt to an AI-driven world; you are equipping them to shape it.

Chapter 7: The Future is Equitable: AI Literacy as a Catalyst for Transformation

As we stand on the precipice of an AI-driven world, we are reminded that this moment is not entirely new. History is rich with examples of transformative technologies that have reshaped societies, altered economies, and redefined what it means to be human. From the printing press to the personal computer, these innovations have opened doors while simultaneously leaving some locked behind. AI, with its immense potential, stands as the next great leap forward—but whether it becomes a tool of inclusion or exclusion is up to us.

The story of literacy offers a clear parallel. Centuries ago, the ability to read and write was not just a skill; it was a symbol of empowerment, a gateway to opportunity, and, for many, a life-altering act of resistance. Today, AI literacy carries the same transformative potential. It has the power to open pathways to economic mobility, civic engagement, and creativity. But like literacy in the past, access to AI is unevenly distributed, threatening to deepen the divides it has the potential to bridge.

This book has urged us to be fearless in imagining a world where AI literacy is the foundation for equity, not another boundary dividing opportunity, essential for equitable participation in society. It has highlighted the systemic inequities that deny marginalized communities access to AI education and the opportunities it represents. Yet, it has also illuminated the possibilities: how AI can be harnessed to amplify human creativity, empower diverse voices, and create a more inclusive world.

AI literacy cannot rest on the shoulders of any single group. Each stakeholder has a role to play in shaping an AI-literate society. Educators can integrate AI into classrooms as a tool for curiosity and critical thinking. Policymakers can advocate for funding and equitable access to technology. Technologists can create tools that reflect the diversity of the communities they serve. Together, these efforts form the foundation of a future where AI serves all, not just a privileged few.

The road ahead is not without obstacles. Systemic inequities in funding, access to devices, and digital infrastructure remain persistent barriers. Ethical challenges, such as bias in AI systems or the potential misuse of AI, add layers of complexity. And yet, the opportunities are equally profound. AI has the capacity to personalize education, amplify creativity, and equip students with the skills needed to navigate a rapidly changing world.

Every challenge is an opportunity in disguise. The lack of access to technology in marginalized communities can be met with advocacy, grants, and partnerships. The ethical pitfalls of AI can become teachable moments, fostering a generation that uses technology responsibly. The rapid pace of AI innovation can inspire adaptable, lifelong learners who are ready to shape, rather than simply respond to, the world around them.

History will judge us not by the technology we create, but by how we choose to wield it. This moment demands bold, transformative action. It is not enough to recognize the importance of AI literacy; we must act on it.

But action does not need to be monumental to be meaningful. A single teacher introducing AI tools into their classroom, a school district applying for grants to bridge the digital divide, a community rallying to bring resources to underserved students—these steps, while small on their own, combine to create ripples of change.

Imagine a world where every child, regardless of their zip code or socioeconomic status, has the tools to understand and shape AI. Picture classrooms where students use AI to solve real-world problems, create art, and innovate in ways we cannot yet imagine. Envision an economy where marginalized voices are not sidelined by technology but amplified through it. This is the future we can build—a future where AI is a bridge, not a barrier.

The first step is always the hardest, but it is also the most important. As you close this book, remember that the power to shape the future lies in the choices we make today. Whether you are an educator, a leader, a parent, or a student, you have a role to play in building a world where AI literacy is not a privilege but a shared foundation for opportunity and justice.

The future is ours to create. Let it be one where AI uplifts, includes, and inspires.

Glossary

AI Bias: Systematic errors in AI systems that can create unfair outcomes for certain groups based on factors like race, gender, or socioeconomic status.

AI Literacy: The ability to understand, critically evaluate, interact with, and ethically engage with artificial intelligence technologies.

Digital Divide: The gap between those who have ready access to computers/internet and those who do not.

Equity: Ensuring fair access, opportunity, and advancement for all people while identifying and eliminating barriers that prevent full participation.

Ghost Policy: Unofficial or unwritten rules about AI use that can affect students differently based on their school's resources or attitudes.

Large Language Models (LLMs): AI systems trained on vast amounts of text data to understand and generate human-like language.

Machine Learning: Systems that can learn and improve from experience without explicit programming.

Marginalized
Refers to individuals or groups that are pushed to the edges of society, economically, socially,

or politically, and are often excluded from full participation in systems of power, decision-making, or opportunity. In the context of this book, it highlights communities that face systemic barriers to accessing education, technology, or economic mobility, such as racial minorities, economically disadvantaged populations, or those without access to digital infrastructure.

Personalized Learning: Education tailored to each student's needs, pace, and learning style, often facilitated by AI.

SHA (Significant Human Authorship): Policy framework for acknowledging and permitting appropriate AI use in student work while maintaining academic integrity.

Technological Empowerment: The ability to not just use technology but to understand, shape, and innovate with it.

Training Data: Information used to teach AI systems, which can reflect and perpetuate societal biases if not carefully curated.

Universal Design for Learning (UDL): Educational framework that can be enhanced by AI to accommodate diverse learning needs.

References

Brookings Institution. (2022). How artificial intelligence will impact K-12 teachers.
Retrieved from https://www.brookings.edu/research/how-artificial-intelligence-will-impact-k-12-teachers/

Common Sense Media. (2020). The digital divide is leaving students behind during the pandemic.
Retrieved from https://www.commonsensemedia.org/research/the-digitaldivide-is-leaving-students-behind-during-the-pandemic

Gregory Kestin*, Kelly Miller*, Anna Klales et al. AI Tutoring Outperforms Active Learning, 14 May 2024, PREPRINT (Version 1) available at Research Square [https://doi.org/10.21203/rs.3.rs-4243877/v1] Microsoft. (2024). 2024 work trend index annual report. https://assets-c4akfrf5b4d3f4b7.z01.azurefd.net/assets/2024

/05/2024_Work_Trend_Index_Annual_Repor
t_6_7_24_666b2e2fafceb.pdf

MIT Technology Review. (2020). The AI bias
problem.
Retrieved from
https://www.technologyreview.com/2020/12/
04/1013068/ai-bias-problem/

National Bureau of Economic Research. (2022).
Exploring 160 years of the Black-White wealth
gap. Retrieved from
https://www.nber.org/digest/202208/explorin
g-160-years-black-white-wealth-gap

Pew Research Center. (2021). The digital divide
persists even as Americans with lower incomes
make gains in tech adoption. Retrieved from
https://www.pewresearch.org/facttank/2021/
06/22/the-digital-divide-persists-even-as-
americans-with-lower-incomesmake-gains-in-
tech-adoption/

World Economic Forum. (2021). The future of
jobs report 2021. Retrieved from

https://www.weforum.org/reports/the-future-of-jobs-report-2021

Note: *While the textual content of this book was crafted entirely by the authors, AI played a role as an editor during the creation process. Additionally, all images featured in this book were generated using AI.*

The views expressed in this work are solely those of the authors and do not reflect the opinions or positions of any affiliated organizations or institutions.